D1506062

CANADA

Julie Murray

VISIT US AT
www.abdopublishing.com

Published by ABDO Publishing Company, PO Box 398166, Minneapolis, MN 55439.

Copyright © 2014 by Abdo Consulting Group, Inc. International copyrights reserved in all countries. No part of this book may be reproduced in any form without written permission from the publisher. Big Buddy Books™ is a trademark and logo of ABDO Publishing Company.

Printed in the United States of America, North Mankato, Minnesota.
042013
092013

 PRINTED ON RECYCLED PAPER

Coordinating Series Editor: Rochelle Baltzer
Editor: Sarah Tieck
Contributing Editors: Megan M. Gunderson, Marcia Zappa
Graphic Design: Adam Craven
Cover Photograph: *Shutterstock*: LaiQuocAnh.
Interior Photographs/Illustrations: *AP Photo*: Alex Brandon (p. 35), Gerry Broome (p. 31), Paul Chiasson (p. 31), Robb Cohen/RobbsPhotos/Invision (p. 33), North Wind Picture Archives via AP Images (pp. 13, 16), The Canadian Press, Ryan Remiorz (p. 17), The Canadian Press, Chris Young (p. 19); *Getty Images*: Scott Olson (p. 5), George Rose (p. 15); *Glow Images*: Kelly Funk (p. 29), JTB Photo (p. 23) Klaus Lang (p. 34), Thompson Paul (p. 27), ARCO/Therin-Weise (p. 29); *iStockphoto*: ©iStockphoto.com/LastSax (p. 38), ©iStockphoto.com/mysticenergy (p. 35), ©iStockphoto.com/SimplyCreativePhotography (p. 25); *Shutterstock*: BGSmith (p. 21), Dolce Vita (p. 25), erdem (pp. 19, 38), steve estvanik (p. 35), Flariviere (p. 27), irisphoto1 (p. 37), Lissandra Melo (p. 9), meunierd (pp. 11, 34), Jeff Whyte (p. 11).

Country population and area figures taken from the CIA World Factbook.

Library of Congress Control Number: 2013932155

Cataloging-in-Publication Data

Murray, Julie.
Canada / Julie Murray.
 p. cm. -- (Explore the countries)
ISBN 978-1-61783-806-4 (lib. bdg.)
1. Canada--Juvenile literature. I. Title.
971--dc23

2013932155

CANADA

Contents

Around the World

Our world has many countries. Each country has different land. It has its own rich history. And, the people have their own languages and ways of life.

Canada is a country in North America. What do you know about Canada? Let's learn more about this place and its story!

Did You Know?

English and French are the official languages of Canada.

The Royal Canadian Mounted Police are famous for their red coats. They are called the "Mounties."

5

PASSPORT TO CANADA

Canada is located in the northern part of North America. The United States is the only country to border it. The Pacific Ocean, Arctic Ocean, and Atlantic Ocean also border Canada.

Canada is the world's second-largest country. Its total area is 3,855,103 square miles (9,984,670 sq km). Canada is split into parts called **provinces** and territories. More than 34.3 million people live there.

WHERE IN THE WORLD?

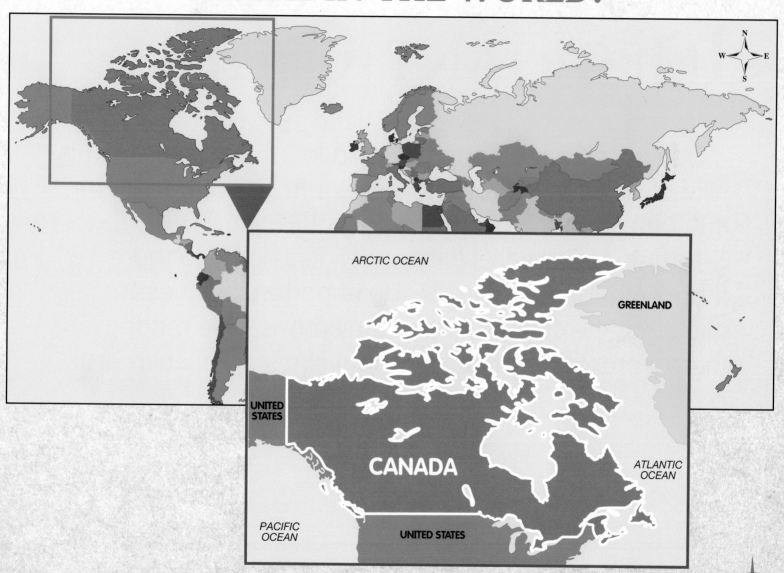

Important Cities

Ottawa is Canada's **capital** and fourth-largest city. This hilly city is on the Ottawa River's south bank. More than 883,000 people live there.

Toronto is Canada's largest city. It is home to more than 2.6 million people. It is an important business center for the country. And, many movies are made there. Toronto hosts an important film festival each year.

SAY IT

Ottawa
AH-tuh-wuh

Toronto
tuh-RAHN-toh

Toronto is located on Lake Ontario. It is home to some of Canada's tallest buildings.

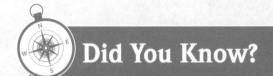

Montreal is Canada's second-largest city. More than 1.6 million people live there. It is known for being on an island. It is also known for education. McGill University and other schools are located there.

Calgary is Canada's third-largest city. It has more than 1 million people. Located at the base of the Canadian Rockies, it is known as Canada's oil center.

SAY IT

Montreal
mahn-tree-AWL

Calgary
KAL-guh-ree

Montreal is home to many old churches called basilicas.

Calgary is a fast-growing modern city.

CANADA IN HISTORY

The first people to live in Canada arrived thousands of years ago from Asia. At that time, a land bridge connected Asia and North America. Later, the Inuit arrived.

Soon, Europeans discovered Canada's valuable **resources**. The French settled there in the 1600s to trade furs. In 1763, Great Britain took control. The people worked to settle the country and use its rich resources.

SAY IT
Inuit *IH-noo-wuht*

The Hudson's Bay Company began as a fur trading business in 1670. It grew into a large and powerful company.

In 1867, Canada formed its own government. The people worked hard to grow its businesses.

Today, Canada is a strong country. It is known for making many products and growing crops. Canada works hard to keep its **provinces** and territories **united**.

Canadians are proud of their country. They celebrate the day Canada became a country on Canada Day. It is July 1.

15

Timeline

1873

The Canadian government formed the Northwest Mounted Police.

1497

Italian explorer John Cabot discovered Canada's rich fishing areas. He was exploring for England. This led to more European exploration of Canada.

1980

The song "O Canada" became Canada's national anthem.

1993

The Montreal Canadiens hockey team won their twenty-fourth Stanley Cup. No other **NHL** team had won more Stanley Cups!

2010

The Winter Olympic Games were held in Vancouver, British Columbia. Canada won the most gold medals!

1982

Great Britain gave Canada control of its **constitution**. This made it a fully independent country.

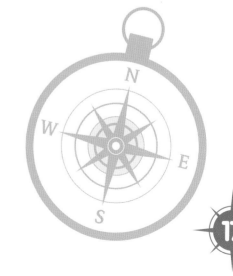

An Important Symbol

Canada's flag was adopted in 1965. It has two red stripes and one white stripe. A red maple leaf is in the center of the white stripe. Canada's official colors are red and white.

Canada's government is a constitutional monarchy. But, it operates as a **federal parliamentary democracy**. The prime minister is the head of government. The United Kingdom's king or queen is the head of state.

The maple leaf stands for Canada.
It is also shown on Canada's penny.

Stephen Joseph Harper became
Canada's prime minister in 2006.

JOBS · GROWTH · PROSPERITY
EMPLOIS · CROISSANCE · PROSPÉRITÉ

CANADA'S ECONOMIC
ACTION PLAN · PLAN D'ACTION

ACROSS THE LAND

Canada is known for its beauty. The Canadian Rockies are a large mountain range in the west. Almost half of the country is covered by forests. Canada also has coasts, glaciers, and islands.

Canada has hundreds of rivers, streams, and lakes. The Great Lakes are located on the border of the United States and Canada. Hudson Bay is another important body of water.

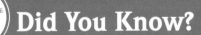

Did You Know?

In July, the average temperature in Ontario is 66°F (19°C). In January, it is about 9°F (-13°C).

Many visitors travel to Canada to spend time in the Rockies. People enjoy camping, hiking, and skiing in these beautiful mountains.

Many types of animals make their homes in Canada. These include moose, bears, and beavers. Fish, walruses, seals, and whales live in the coastal waters.

Canada's land is home to many different plants. These include maple, oak, and birch trees. There are also jack pines and spruce trees, as well as mosses and grasses. Part of Canada is **tundra**. There, it is too cold and dry for trees to grow.

Animals such as polar bears live in Canada's tundra. Their bodies are made for living in Arctic conditions.

Earning a Living

Canada is known for its strong businesses. Many people have health care, education, or legal jobs. Others have jobs helping visitors. The country's factories make cars, airplanes, and food products.

Canada has many natural **resources**. Gold, nickel, and stone are mined there. Farmers produce wheat, barley, fruits, and vegetables. Fish, lobster, and shrimp come from Canada's waters.

Ontario produces more cars than any US state. And, Quebec has one of the world's largest airplane makers.

Canada is a world leader in oil production.

LIFE IN CANADA

Most Canadians live in modern cities. Cities are home to art and history museums and libraries. Much music and many movies and books are made in Canada.

Foods in Canada are like those in the United States. Canada is known for making maple syrup. This is eaten on pancakes and waffles. *Poutine* is a popular dish that includes French fries, gravy, and cheese.

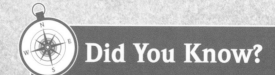

Did You Know?

In Canada, schools are run by the provinces and territories. Most children attend 12 grades, or levels, of school.

Native Americans from Canada's west coast are known for their wood carvings and totem poles. Some are displayed in the country's museums.

Maple syrup is made from the sap of certain maple trees.

Canadians enjoy sports. Ice hockey is very popular. Other favorites include baseball, football, and curling. People spend time outside skiing and ice skating. They may also hike or fish in natural areas.

Many Native American groups live in Canada. The Inuit people live in the Arctic. Most live like other modern Canadians. But, some still use dogsleds and kayaks. Many speak the Inuit language. And, they show their history and traditions in art and storytelling.

Curling is played on a sheet of ice. Players slide stones across the ice toward a tee, or button.

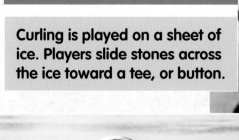

 Did You Know?

Canada has hosted the Olympic Games three times.

Some styles of clothing came from the Inuit people. These include parkas and animal furs.

29

FAMOUS FACES

Canada is known for hockey. Wayne Gretzky is a famous player. He was born on January 26, 1961, in Brantford, Ontario.

Gretzky played in the **NHL** from 1979 to 1999. Many people call him "the Great One." He scored more goals than any other NHL player. After retiring, Gretzky worked as a **coach**.

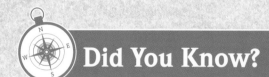

Did You Know?

Gretzky was the first to win the Hart Memorial Trophy eight years in a row. This award goes to the NHL player believed to be most valuable to his team.

In 1999, Gretzky was added to the Hockey Hall of Fame.

Gretzky was honored to carry the 2010 Olympic torch.

Many music stars have come from Canada, too. Justin Bieber was born on March 1, 1994, in Stratford, Ontario.

In 2007, Bieber and his mom began to post videos of him singing on YouTube. Soon, Bieber was discovered and moved to the United States. His first album, *My World*, came out in 2009. It was a hit! He continued to grow more successful.

Did You Know?

Other well-known Canadian musicians include Leonard Cohen, Michael Bublé, Céline Dion, Shania Twain, and Bryan Adams.

In 2012 and 2013, Bieber toured North America. He sang songs from his album *Believe*.

33

Tour Book

Have you ever been to Canada? If you visit the country, here are some places to go and things to do!

See

Spend time in Montreal's Mount Royal Park. People often ice skate on Beaver Lake in winter. They also visit high spots to look out over the city.

Watch

Take in some of William Shakespeare's plays. The Stratford Shakespeare Festival is held every summer in Stratford.

 # Explore

Hike in Jasper National Park. People travel there and throughout Canada to spend time in mountains and forests.

 # Cheer

Watch the Montreal Canadiens play hockey. It is the most successful team in the history of the NHL.

 # Play

Hang out at the Calgary Stampede. Held every July, this world-famous event includes shows and a rodeo.

A Great Country

The story of Canada is important to our world. The people and places that make up this country offer something special. They help make the world a more beautiful, interesting place.

Banff National Park is in Alberta. It officially became Canada's first national park in 1887.

Canada Up Close

Official Name: Canada

Flag:

Population (rank): 34,300,083
(July 2012 est.)
(35th most-populated country)

Total Area (rank): 3,855,103 square miles
(2nd largest country)

Capital: Ottawa

Official Languages: English, French

Currency: Canadian dollar

Forms of Government: Constitutional monarchy and federal parliamentary democracy

National Anthem: "O Canada"

Important Words

capital a city where government leaders meet.
coach someone who teaches or trains a person or a group on a certain subject or skill.
constitution the basic laws that govern a country or a state.
federal parliamentary democracy a government in which the power is held by the people, who exercise it by voting. It is run by a cabinet whose members belong to the legislature. The central government and the individual provinces share power.
NHL National Hockey League. The NHL is a group of ice hockey teams in the United States and Canada.
province a large section within a country, like a state.
resource a supply of something useful or valued.
tundra flat, frozen Arctic land with no trees.
unite to come together for purpose or action.

Web Sites

To learn more about Canada, visit ABDO Publishing Company online. Web sites about Canada are featured on our Book Links page. These links are routinely monitored and updated to provide the most current information available.

www.abdopublishing.com

Index